I0620798

This book belongs to

_____

Dedication

This is book is dedicated to my beloved children, nieces and nephews and to all the parents and young dreamers. May this book bring you joy, love and blessings.

What is Eid?

Let's start with the meaning of the word 'Eid'!
Eid is an Arabic word that means a special celebration. It is a happy day for Muslims.
Muslims celebrate two special festivals called Eid! The first one is Eid Al-Fitr, which comes after Ramadaan. The second is Eid Al-Adha, which happens after Hajj. Let's learn more about both Eids together!

Eid Al-Fitr is after Ramadaan and means the festival of breaking the fast.

Eid Al-Adha is after Hajj and means the festival of the sacrifice.

Eid Al-Fitr

After Ramadaan, we celebrate Eid Al-Fitr because Ramadaan has come to an end. Eid is a happy time! We pray special prayers, enjoy delicious food with family and friends, and share with those in need. Come along and discover the special Eid traditions and Sunnah!

Let's get ready for our Eid prayer!

To get ready for the Eid prayer, we start by performing Ghusl, a special shower. This is something our beloved Prophet (peace be upon him) recommended. Then, we wear our most beautiful clothes and put on our best perfume— boys can wear it anywhere, while girls wear it only at home. Some girls may have a special dress (abaya) for the mosque and a different one for home. Many people also love wearing their cultural clothing on this special day.

What is your favourite outfit to wear?

1. *Shower (Ghusl)*

2. *Wear my best perfume (boys)*

3. *Wear my special Eid clothes*

On the morning of Eid al-Fitr, it's a special tradition to eat dates before going to the prayer. But there's something special about the way we eat them—we eat them in odd numbers!

The Prophet Muhammad (peace be upon him) used to eat 1, 3, or 5 dates before leaving for the prayer. It's a way of following his example and showing thanks for the month of fasting.

So, on Eid, we enjoy a little treat of dates, in an odd number, to feel happy and ready for the fun celebrations ahead!
On the way to the Eid prayer, we say the Takbeer to praise Allah.

We say:
"Allahu Akbar, Allahu Akbar, la ilaha illa Allah, Allahu Akbar, Allahu Akbar wa lillahil-hamd."
Can you practice saying the Takbeer with a big smile?

Eid Al-Adha

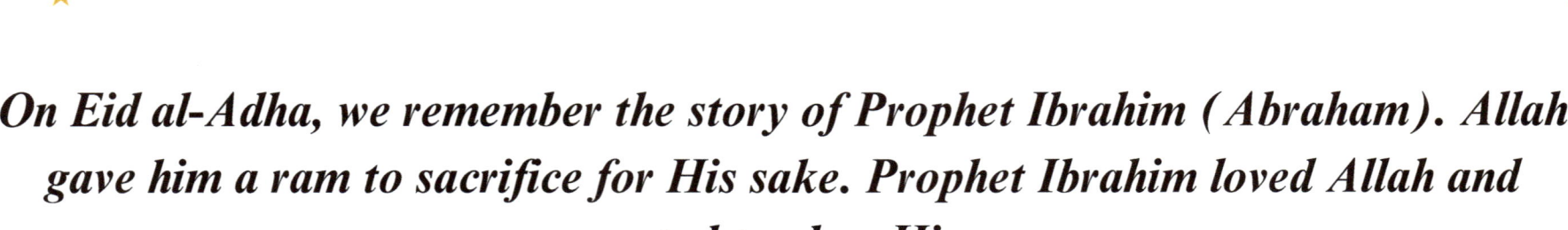

On Eid al-Adha, we remember the story of Prophet Ibrahim (Abraham). Allah gave him a ram to sacrifice for His sake. Prophet Ibrahim loved Allah and wanted to obey Him.
Ever since then, Muslims have followed this tradition.

On this special day, many families sacrifice an animal like a sheep or goat. This meat is shared with family, friends, and people in need. It teaches us to be generous and to give to those who may not have enough.

Eid al-Adha is also a time for prayer, celebration, and thanking Allah for all the blessings we have.
Can you think of anything we can share with others on Eid to show kindness and love?

IBRAHIM

On Eid day, after the special Eid prayer, the Prophet Muhammad (peace be upon him) would do something special—he would take a different path home!

Why did he do this?
✨ *So he could greet more people and spread joy.*
✨ *To show thankfulness for this happy day.*
✨ *To earn more rewards by walking different paths.*

Eid is a time for smiles, kindness, and sharing happiness!
Can you think of a new way to walk home on Eid, just like the Prophet (peace be upon him) did?

After the Eid prayer, some of us will go home to enjoy some delicious food and open presents! And we might also visit family and friends to share a special meal together.

What is your favorite Eid treat to eat?"

The meaning of the Eid Takbeer

Allahu Akbar, Allahu Akbar, Laa ilaha illa Allah. Allahu Akbar, Allahu Akbar wa Lillahi alhamd.

Allah is the greatest, Allah is the greatest, there is no god but Allah, and Allah is the greatest, Allah is the greatest and all praise belongs to Allah.

The End
Eid Mubarak!

Acknowledgements

I would like to thank my mother who has always been an inspiration to me, for believing in me and supporting me. Thank you, mom!

A special thank you to my husband for the endless support.

I would like to thank one of our dear friends, Mr. R.T. Richards, who has given me valuable insight and feedback on this lovely book.

About the Author

Sakina is a half Moroccan half Dutch mother of three who is passionate about creating stories that inspire and delight young readers. With a background in childhood education, parenting and storytelling, she enjoys crafting books that spark imagination and education to foster a love for reading. As a parent and former teaching assistant Sakina understands the joy of sharing meaningful stories with children. When not writing Sakina enjoys spending time with her family, being in nature or reading with her children.

www.ingramcontent.com/pod-product-compliance
Lightning Source LLC
Chambersburg PA
CBHW040815120626

46547CB00005B/553